We Use Water

by Margie Burton, Cathy French, and Tammy Jones

We use water
to drink.

We use water
for washing clothes.

We use water
to clean our hands.

The firemen

can use water, too.

We use water
for cooking.

We use water
to wash the car.

We use water
for the plants.

We use water
to have fun.